Welsh Retrospective

Dannie Abse
Welsh Retrospective

seren

Seren is the book imprint of
Poetry Wales Press Ltd
Nolton Street, Bridgend, Wales, CF31 3AE
www.serenbooks.com

First published 1997
This edition 2008, reprinted 2010, 2011, 2012
Poems © Dannie Abse
Introduction and Notes © Cary Archard

ISBN 978-1-85411-486-0

A CIP record for this title is available from the British Library

*The publisher works with the financial assistance of
the Welsh Books Council*

Cover illustration: 'Dinas/Settlement' by Iwan Bala
reproduced by permission of The Sound Works

Printed by Short Run Press, Exeter

CONTENTS

INTRODUCTION

In 1943 Dannie Abse left Cardiff, where he had grown up, and went to London to continue his medical studies. Once qualified he married, then lived and worked in London. This has not been an unfamiliar life pattern: for most of this century many Welsh men and women have moved out of Wales to work, only returning for holidays or family weddings and funerals. However, this pattern does not really fit Dannie Abse's story. Although he may have worked at a chest clinic in London, he has never actually stopped living in Wales. The views from the Paddington-Cardiff railway line and from the M4 have been for him regular experiences, as prominent a part of his visual imagination as his Golders Green garden, or the Bristol Channel from his Welsh home at Ogmore-by-Sea. Significantly, many of those journeys have culminated in Ninian Park, home to the Bluebirds, the Cardiff City football team he has devotedly followed since boyhood and where he is still a season ticket holder.

This selected poems, which collects together most of the poems Dannie Abse has written directly about Wales, is important for a number of reasons. To begin with, it represents the remarkable continuity of the poet's life and writing: the poems, including one of his earliest, 'Leaving Cardiff', are taken from most of his volumes up to his most recent, *Running Late* (2006), and also include a number of poems which have not previously been published in book form. This selection shows the central importance of Dannie Abse's Welsh and Jewish childhood to his poetic concerns. It is a subject that he comes back to constantly, not just here but in his popular prose writings too. Cardiff, that fair city where he grew up, has to a large extent been his muse: although (perhaps because) he has travelled a lot, it is a place he has never wanted to let go of.

Secondly, the book celebrates memory: "Carmi said ... thank memory, else we'd have no life" ('A Letter from Ogmore'). It is as though living outside Wales as well as inside has sharpened memory, the faculty the traveller lives by. Dannie Abse remembers not only his closest relatives (mother, father, grandmothers, aunts and uncles) but also a wider Welsh "family" of idolised footballers and cricketers, his not-so-revered music teacher and his great Welsh poet predecessors, Dylan Thomas and Vernon Watkins – these latter in poems which even evoke the idiosyncratic styles of these writers. A remarkable number of the selected poems are elegies or epitaphs, but the poems are not so much about death as about those who have died. Looking back, remembering Wales, Dannie Abse is unfailingly accompanied by ghosts.

This book is important also for what it reveals of Dannie Abse's indebtedness to Welsh language forms and Welsh literature and history. Making this kind of selection allows us to see the importance of this aspect of his work. Although his mother was a Welsh speaker, the language was heard infrequently at home and Dannie Abse did not learn Welsh like R.S. Thomas or many of the younger English language poets of Wales. The occasionally strident nationalism of some of these poets is absent from his work. Instead he pays a poet's homage to the older language of Wales and its traditions, in poems such as 'Meurig Dafydd to His Mistress', a vivid creation of the seventeenth century bard Meurig Dafydd's delightfully ribald attack on the English poet John Stradling, and in his atmospheric versions of Heledd's 'Lament' and Hywel's 'Boasts'. These poems develop another form of continuity: besides recalling his childhood and remembering his family, Dannie Abse replays the tunes of earlier Welsh poets. This *Retrospective* contributes to a particularly *Welsh* tradition.

That absence makes the heart grow fonder is a cliché but nonetheless true. Driving down the M4 to visit his mother in Cardiff, Dannie Abse whistles "an old Yiddish tune", one his "mother knows", but the poem itself gives us more loudly the song of the river Tawe which "ran fluent and trout-coloured over stones stonier, more genuine". Dannie Abse's Welsh poems in particular sing of the "genuine". That adjective means "from the original stock; real, true, authentic; sincere, not assumed." It seems to characterise much of his Wales, as in the striking and unusual poem 'A Wall' which is not about childhood, Cardiff or travelling. The wall seems out of place, this "unremarkable wall", "in a field in the county of Glamorgan". The poet urges us not to "say this wall is useless". He is drawn to it because it goes nowhere, because it seemingly has no purpose. But the wall is *genuine* and it does have a role; it shelters sheep and butterflies, lichen grows on it. Above all it exists "for you to say, 'This wall is beautiful'." It might also be the place to start to understand Dannie Abse's poems about Wales.

Cary Archard

Leaving Cardiff

I wait in the evening air.
Sea-birds drop down to the sea.
I prepare to sail from where
the docks' derelictions are.

I stand on the deck and stare,
slack hammocks of waves below,
while black shapes upon the pier
make the furthest star seem near.

Now the funnel's negations blow
and my eyes, like spaces, fill,
and the knots of water flow,
pump to my eyes and spill.

For what *who* would choose to go
when *who* sailing made no choice?
Not for one second, I know,
can I be the same man twice.

The straw coloured flames flare still,
spokes over the long horizon,
and the boats under the hill
of Penarth unload and move on.

Musical Moments

1. His Last Piano Lesson (1933)

'Poet, be seated at the piano.' – Wallace Stevens

When, after tea,
(Germany still six million
miles away) Miss Crouch,
the upright piano teacher,
knocks at the front door
the boy's at the back door.
Numbly bored with scales
nimbly scales the wall

and hearing in the park
the pointless cries of children,
joins butter-fingered Jack
and his high-flung tennis ball.

There backslangs
and jabberwocks,
swaps acid-drops for bull's-eyes,
Hammond for Hobbs,
and one pocket-aged
PK chewing gum —

till the park-keeper comes
stamping the gravel path,
blowing his whistle,
making the sparrows fly
from their scattered park bench crumbs
(their little noise
the shaking of umbrellas).

Back home, downstairs,
the piano-lid's closed,
a coffin of music.
Their war-faces, their big thumbs.

Exiguous memory:
Remembrance of Crimes Past, 1933,
so few and so many!
On the sideboard,
walnuts in a cut-glass bowl,
and the father raging,
'That's his last piano lesson.'

O joy, Miss dismissed!

Later, only the landing light
under the bedroom door:
no hectoring voices,
no blameless man-sized scarecrow
being thumped down the carpeted stairs

before Sleep's grisly fictions
and forgeries of the world.

2. Outside a Graveyard (1989)

> *'One day, the piano has all the colours of the orchestra; another*
> *day, it brings forth sounds that come from other worlds.'*
> *– Edwin Fischer*

Many nearer than you have gone, too many,
so your going does not touch me deeply,
a one-fingered piano note only,
soft as a caress, sounding regret
and then again regret, diminuendo,
spare – hardly a Wagnerian Funeral March;
yet I want to say, 'Sorry, Miss Crouch,'
now that you are dismissed forever.
You were so unassuming and gentle.
If there's a heaven, that's your address.

Once, after the war, I observed you
at a romantic Moiseiwitsch concert,
at Cardiff's plush Empire (so soon after

demolished, replaced by a neon-lit superstore).
You sat thrilled in the stalls, eyes raptly shut
– not in the insanity of prayer but
as if that music was making love to you.

Now I stare at church gargoyles, church spire,
then close my eyes also. Wait! Be patient! Look!
The Assumption of Miss Crouch. There! Up there!
Several hundred feet above the spire,
blessed and sedate in evening dress,
rising slowly above Glamorganshire,
you, old lady, playing the piano –
not an upright piece of furniture either
but a concert-hall, exalted Bechstein,
its one black wing uplifted and beating,
bringing forth sounds from another world,
yes, you and the piano triumphantly rising
between the clouds, higher and higher.

Horse

You can't quite
identify it
the long straight road
unsignposted
zipping between hedges
to a scandalously
gorgeous sunset.
As you look closer
shading your eyes
with your right hand
vigilant you'll see
the visitant
the white horse
half way down it.

Do you remember?
Your father drove the car
the family squabbling
this way years ago
many a time
this Roman road
that's empty now
but for the distant
truant pink horse
with a barely
visible
red shadow
racing towards
the signals of sunset.

War-high in the sky
vapour trails fatten
and you know again
the common sense
of *déjà vu*. Perhaps
someone far from home
should be playing
a mouth organ
a melody slow

and sad and wanton
a tune you've heard
but can't quite say
as the purple horse
surprises the sunset.

And you close your eyes
trying to name it all.
But you recall only
the day's small prose
certain queachy things
what the office said
what the office did
as the sunset goes
as the black horse goes
into the darkness.
And you forget
how from the skin
below your thumbnail
your own moon rises.

Red Balloon

It sailed across the startled town,
over chapels, over chimney-pots,
wind-blown above a block of flats
before it floated down.

Oddly, it landed where I stood,
and finding's keeping, as you know.
I breathed on it, I polished it,
till it shone like living blood.

It was my shame, it was my joy,
it brought me notoriety.
From all of Wales the rude boys came,
it ceased to be a toy.

I heard the girls of Cardiff sigh
when my balloon, my red balloon,
soared higher like a happiness
towards the dark blue sky.

Nine months since, have I boasted of
my unique, my only precious;
but to no one dare I show it now
however long they swear their love.

'It's a Jew's balloon,' my best friend cried,
'stained with our dear Lord's blood.'
'That I'm a Jew is true,' I said,
said I, 'that cannot be denied.'

'What relevance?' I asked, surprised,
'what's religion to do with this?'
'Your red balloon's a Jew's balloon,
let's get it circumcised.'

Then some boys laughed and some boys cursed,
some unsheathed their dirty knives;
some lunged, some clawed at my balloon,
but still it would not burst.

They bled my nose, they cut my eye,
half conscious in the street I heard,
'Give up, give up your red balloon.'
I don't know exactly why.

Father, bolt the door, turn the key,
lest those sad, brash boys return
to insult my faith and steal
my red balloon from me.

Down the M4

Me! dutiful son going back to South Wales, this time
    afraid
to hear my mother's news. Too often, now, her friends
    are disrobed,
and my aunts and uncles, too, go into the hole, one by
    one.
The beautiful face of my mother is in its ninth decade.

Each visit she tells me the monotonous story of clocks.
'Oh dear,' I say, or 'how funny,' till I feel my hair
    turning grey
for I've heard that perishable one two hundred times
    before –
like the rugby 'amateurs' with golden sovereigns in their
    socks.

Then the Tawe ran fluent and trout-coloured over
    stones stonier,
more genuine; then Annabella, my mother's mother,
    spoke Welsh
with such an accent the village said, 'Tell the truth,
    fach,
you're no Jewess. *They're* from the Bible. *You're* from
    Patagonia!'

I'm driving down the M4 again under bridges that leap
over me, then shrink in my side mirror. Ystalyfera is
    farther
than smoke and God further than all distance known.
    I whistle
no hymn but an old Yiddish tune my mother knows.
    It won't keep.

Return to Cardiff

'Hometown'; well, most admit an affection for a city:
grey, tangled streets I cycled on to school, my first
    cigarette
in the back lane, and, fool, my first botched love affair.
First everything. Faded torments; self-indulgent pity.

The journey to Cardiff seemed less a return than a raid
on mislaid identities. Of course the whole locus smaller:
the mile-wide Taff now a stream, the castle not as in
    some black,
gothic dream, but a decent sprawl, a joker's toy façade.

Unfocused voices in the wind, associations, clues,
odds and ends, fringes caught, as when, after the doctor
    quit,
a door opened and I glimpsed the white, enormous face
of my grandfather, suddenly aghast with certain news.

Unable to define anything I can hardly speak,
and still I love the place for what I wanted it to be
as much as for what it unashamedly is
now for me, a city of strangers, alien and bleak.

Unable to communicate I'm easily betrayed,
uneasily diverted by mere sense reflections
like those anchored waterscapes that wander, alter, in
    the Taff,
hour by hour, as light slants down a different shade.

Illusory, too, that lost dark playground after rain,
the noise of trams, gunshots in what they once called
    Tiger Bay.
Only real this smell of ripe, damp earth when the sun
    comes out,
a mixture of pungencies, half exquisite and half plain.

No sooner than I'd arrived the other Cardiff had gone,
smoke in the memory, these but tinned resemblances,
where the boy I was not and the man I am not
met, hesitated, left double footsteps, then walked on.

The Game

Follow the crowds to where the turnstiles click.
The terraces fill. *Hoompa,* blares the brassy band.
Saturday afternoon has come to Ninian Park
and, beyond the goal posts, in the Canton Stand
between black spaces, a hundred matches spark.

Waiting, we recall records, legendary scores:
Fred Keenor, Hardy, in a royal blue shirt.
The very names, sad as the old songs, open doors
before our time where someone else was hurt.
Now, like an injured beast, the great crowd roars.

The coin is spun. Here all is simplified,
and we are partisan who cheer the Good,
hiss at passing Evil. Was Lucifer offside?
A wing falls down when cherubs howl for blood.
Demons have agents: the Referee is bribed.

The white ball smacked the crossbar. Satan rose
higher than the others in the smoked brown gloom
to sink on grass in a ballet dancer's pose.
Again, it seems, we hear a familiar tune
not quite identifiable. A distant whistle blows.

Memory of faded games, the discarded years;
talk of Aston Villa, Orient, and the Swans.
Half-time, the band played the same military airs
as when the Bluebirds once were champions.
Round touchlines the same cripples in their chairs.

Mephistopheles had his joke. The honest team
dribbles ineffectively, no one can be blamed.
Infernal backs tackle, inside forwards scheme,
and if they foul us need we be ashamed?
Heads up! Oh for a Ted Drake, a Dixie Dean.

'Saved' or else, discontents, we are transferred
long decades back, like Faust must pay that fee.
The night is early. Great phantoms in us stir

as coloured jerseys hover, move diagonally
on the damp turf, and our eidetic visions blur.

God sign our souls! Because the obscure staff
of Hell rule this world, jugular fans guessed
the result halfway through the second half,
and those who know the score just seem depressed.
Small boys swarm the field for an autograph.

Silent the stadium. The crowds have all filed out.
Only the pigeons beneath the roofs remain.
The clean programmes are trampled underfoot,
and natural the dark, appropriate the rain,
whilst, under lampposts, threatening newsboys shout.

Cricket Ball

1935, I watched Glamorgan play
especially Slogger Smart, free
from the disgrace of fame, unrenowned,
but the biggest hit with me.

A three-spring flash of willow
and suddenly, the sound of summer
as the thumped ball, alive, would leave
the applauding ground.

Once, hell for leather, it curled
over the workman's crane
in Westgate Street
to crash, they said, through a discreet
Angel Hotel windowpane.

But I, a pre-war boy,
(or someone with my name)
wanted it, that Eden day,
to scoot around the turning world,
to mock physics and gravity,
to rainbow-arch the posh hotel
higher, deranged, on and on, allegro,
(the Taff a gleam of mercury below)
going, going, gone
towards the Caerphilly mountain range.

Vanishings! The years, too, gone like change.
But the travelling Taff seems the same.
It's late. I peer at the failing sky
over Westgate Street
and wait. I smell cut grass.
I shine an apple on my thigh.

Welsh Valley Cinema, 1930s

In The Palace of the slums,
from the Saturday night pit,
from an unseen shaft of darkness
I remember it: how, first, a sound
took wing grandly; then the thrill
of a fairground sight — it rose,
lordly stout thing, boasting
a carnival of gaudy-bright,
changing colours while wheezing out
swelling ronchi of musical asthma.

I hear it still, played with panache
by renowned gent, Cathedral Jones,
'When the Broadway Baby Says Goodnight
it's Early in the Morning' – then he and it
sank to disappear, a dream underground.

Later, those downstairs, gobbing silicosis
(shoeless feet on the mecca carpet),
observed a miracle – the girl next door,
a poor ragged Goldilocks,
dab away her glycerine tears
to kiss cuff-linked Cary Grant
under an elegance of chandeliers.
(No flies on Cary. No holes in *his* socks.)

And still the Woodbine smoke swirled on
in the opium beam of the operator's box
till THE END – of course, upbeat.
Then from The Palace, the damned Fall,
the glum, too silent trooping out
into the trauma of paradox:
the familiar malice of the dreary,
unemployed, gas-lamped street
and the striking of the small Town's clocks.

Arianrhod

Not Arianrhod of Swansea
who could have become a nun,
not cold-flame Arianrhod?
Once, near poppydrowsing corn,
through the cricket weather
consentiently together;
but twice the quarrels after,
dissonances and disorder,
eye-bright denunciations
from theological Arianrhod,
disinclined Arianrhod,
while two rivers were meeting
at Pontneathvaughan.

Night-war came to Swansea
when the kettle was whistling,
Bowdler lay deeper
in Mumbles' graveyard.
Hurdling fire turned to fire
the things it first charred —
both gone Arianrhod's parents
who wailed with the siren,
that ghost-factory siren;
and later stunned Arianrhod
diminished in hospital,
tongue-rotted in hospital,
because their going was hard.

Do names have destinies?
Today in a chronic ward
another Arianrhod, a schizophrene,
picking the frost from her face.
Then back down the landing
heard myself mumbling – Destiny
itself is a man-made name.
Out through the front gate
but still see her standing
on light-iced linoleum,
that used one, Arianrhod,
figure a matchstick,
flame gone without trace.

Lament of Heledd

(based on a fragment of a ninth century Welsh saga poem)

I

I had four brothers. A pike upholds the head
of noble Cynddylan. The corn is red.

I had four brothers. Cynon and Gwiawn
butchered in the straw, their swords not drawn.

Four brothers I had. Vague, hesitant Gwyn
last to fall. Through his neck a javelin.

When will this brute night end? Where shall I go?
Morning's mortuary will be kitchen for the crow.

II

   Cynddylan's Hall is dark tonight.
The stone stairs lead nowhere. No candle glows
behind the lower then the higher windows.

   Cynddylan's Hall is dark tonight
and dark the smoke rising from its ruin.
Slain, slain, is Cynddylan and all our kin.

   Cynddylan's Hall is dark tonight,
its great roof burnt down, I can see the stars.
Curse those Englishmen, their bloody wars.

   Cynddylan's Hall is dark tonight.
No orison is wailed to harp or lute.
O ghost brothers, your sister's destitute.

   Cynddylan's Hall is dark tonight,
its silence outrageous. I shall go mad.
I smell skeletons. O blood of my blood.

Cynddylan's hall is dark tonight.
Should I live on? I am no heroine.
O Cynddylan, Cynon, Gwiawn, and Gwyn.

The Boasts of Hywel ab Owain Gwynedd
(Twelfth century)

Sunday, skilled in zealous verse I praise the Lord.
Monday, I sing in bed to my busty Nest,
'Such whiteness you are, pear blossom must be jealous.'
Tuesday, scholar Gwladus. Not to love her is a sin.
My couplets *she* pigeon-coos when I thrust to woo her
till her pale cheeks flush like rosy apple skin.
Wednesday, Generys. Dry old hymns I steal to please
    her.
Then with passion fruit in season I kneel to ease her.
Thursday, Hunydd, no hesitating lady, she.
One small cherry-englyn and she's my devotee.
Friday, worried Hawis, my epic regular.
She wants no baby, she's gooseberry vehement
till sugared by my poetry of endearment.
Saturday, I score and score. One tidy eulogy
and I'm away – I can't brake – through an orchard
I adore. O sweet riot of efflorescence,
let her name be secret for her husband's sake,
my peach of a woman, my vegetarian diet.

O tongue, lick up juices of the fruit. O teeth
– I've all of mine – be sure my busy tongue keeps
    quiet.

Meurig Dafydd to His Mistress

No word I huffed when Stradling urged the squire
to throw my eulogy on the fire.
The fiddlers laughed. I, snow-silent, proud,
did not melt. But I'm spitless now,
my pearl, my buttercup, my bread-fruit.
I rattle their silver in my pocket.
I have other stanzas for harp and lute,
other gullible lords to flatter.
What do I care for that big-bellied Englishman,
that bugle, that small-beer, that puff-ball,
that dung-odoured sonneteer, John Stradling?

Does he sing perfect metre like Taliesin?
Not that gout-toed, goat-faced manikin.
What does he know of Welsh necks crayoned
by the axe, blood on our feet, our history?
Has he stood pensive at the tomb
of Morien, or Morial, or March?
Wept at any nervous harp, at the gloom
of a dirge for Llywelyn the Last,
or the lament by Lewis Glyn Cothi?
That fungoid, that bunt, that broken-wind,
that bog-bean, can't tell a song from a grunt.

Clean heart, my theology, my sweet-briar,
he'd put out heritage on the fire.
Each night he swigs mead in a safe bed –
never sleeps roofed only by the stars.
At noon, never signs the euphonious nine
sermons of the blackbird. O my lotus,
his lexicon is small compared to mine.

His verses are like standing urine – tepid.
My Welsh stanzas have more heat in them
than the tumbling flames in the fire-place
of the Minstrel Hall of Bewpyr.

Elegy for Dylan Thomas

All down the valleys they are talking,
and in the community of the smoke-laden town.
Tomorrow, through bird-trailed skies, across labouring
        waves,
wrong-again Emily will come to the dandelion yard
    and, with rum tourists, inspect his grave.

    Death was his voluntary marriage,
and his poor silence sold to that rich and famous bride.
    Beleaguered in that essential kiss he rode
the whiskey-meadows of her breath till, mortal, voiceless,
    he gave up his nailed ghost and he died.

    No more to celebrate
his disinherited innocence or your half-buried heart
    drunk as a butterfly, or sober as black.
Now, one second from earth, not even for the sake
    of love can his true energy come back.

    So cease your talking.
Too familiar you blaspheme his name and collected legends:
    some tears fall soundlessly and aren't the same
    as those that drop with obituary explosions.
    Suddenly, others who sing seem older and lame.

    But far from the blind country of prose,
wherever his burst voice goes about you or through you,
    look up in surprise, in a hurt public house
    or in a rain-blown street, and see how
    no fat ghost but a quotation cries.

    Stranger, he is laid to rest
not in the nightingale dark nor in the canary light.
    At the dear last, the yolk broke in his head,
    blood of his soul's egg in a splash of bright
    voices and now he is dead.

A Sea-shell for Vernon Watkins

A stage moon and you, too, unreal, unearthed.
Then two shadows athletic down the cliffs
of Pennard near the nightshift of the sea.
You spoke of Yeats and Dylan, your sonorous
pin-ups. I thought, *relentless romantic!*
Darkness stayed in a cave and I lifted
a sea-shell from your shadow when you big-talked
how the dead resume the silence of God.

The bank calls in its debts and all are earthed.
Only one shadow at Pennard today
and listening to another sea-shell I found,
startled, its phantom sea utterly silent
– the shell's cochlea scooped out. Yet appropriate
that small void, that interruption of sound,
for what should be heard in a shell at Pennard
but the stopped breath of a poet who once sang loud?

Others gone also, like you dispensable,
famed names once writ in gold on spines of books
now rarely opened, the young asking, 'Who?'
The beaches of the world should be strewn with such
dumb shells while the immortal sea syllables
in self-love its own name, 'Sea, Sea, Sea, Sea.'
I turn to leave Pennard. This shell is useless.
If I could cry I would but not for you.

A Heritage

A heritage of a sort.
A heritage of comradeship and suffocation.

The bawling pit-hooter and the god's
explosive foray, vengeance, before retreating
to his throne of sulphur.

Now this black-robed god of fossils
and funerals,
petrifier of underground forests
and flowers,
emerges with his grim retinue
past a pony's skeleton, past human skulls,
into his half-propped up, empty, carbon colony.

Above, on the brutalised,
unstitched side of a Welsh mountain,
it has to be someone from somewhere else
who will sing solo

not of the marasmus of the Valleys,
the pit-wheels that do not turn,
the pump-house abandoned;

nor of how, after a half-mile fall,
regiments of miners' lamps
no longer, midge-like,
rise and slip and bob.

Only someone uncommitted,
someone from somewhere else,
panorama-high on a coal-tip,
may jubilantly laud
the re-entry of the exiled god
into his shadowless kingdom.

He, drunk with methane,
raising a man's femur like a sceptre;
she, his ravished queen,
admiring the blood-stained black roses
that could not thrive on the plains of Enna.

An Old Commitment

Long ago my kinsmen slain in battle,
swart flies on all their pale masks feeding.

I had a cause then. Surely I had a cause?
I was for them and they were for me.

Now, when I recall why, what, who,
I think the thought that is as blank as stone.

Travelling this evening, I focus on the back
of brightness, on that red spot wavering.

Behind it, what have I forgotten? It goes
where the red spot goes, rising, descending.

I only describe a sunset, a car travelling
on a swerving mountain road, that's all.

Arriving too late, I approach the unlit dark.
Those who loiter outside exits and entrances

so sadly, so patiently, even they have departed.
And I am no ghost and this place is in ruins.

'Black,' I call softly to one dead but beloved,
'black, black,' wanting the night to reply ...

                                    ... 'Black.'

Altercation in Splott

Before the frosted window is shattered,
immigrant, touch stone and be lucky.

Widower, Sunil, calls most men, 'Sir'.
Hindu pacifist, chanter of prayers.

Cold and cloned, the next door room to his:
bed, chair, threadbare carpet, vertical

fat coffin with a keyhole in it,
damp stain of almost Wales on the wall,

inert with the slow interminable
silence of a broken radio

till volcano-loud, football hooligan
Darren Jones big-boots in. Me? Racialist?

Nah. Politics is shit, mun. On the stairs
I smiles back at the Paki, see.

But rust sleeps within the iron.
One night, pub closed, Darren's jugular.

Paki, you wanker, stop chantin', Christ!
Nothin' much, see. Bust 'is 'ead in a bit

that's all. No shit under the door like.
Righteous as a Town Hall, Darren Jones.

One winter week's notice for bleak Sunil.
Never complain to a blue-eyed landlord.

Ice is on the pond. Swan is on the snow.
But far from the neighbourhood of parks,

Sunil, long-armed, suitcase in each hand,
treads past the depot on pavements' linen,

seems, in sleet-mist, more a conjuration
than a man. Indian out of season.

Sir, stone fall on jug: woe.
Sir, jug falls on stone: woe.

Assimilation

Even the Sodomites, I said, would allow
distraught refugees into their desert city,
provide them with a Sodom-made bed.

But strangers too tall, it must be admitted,
had their legs chopped off; and nationalistic Sods
heaved at heads and feet of those too small
till beds and bodies beautifully fitted.

The Mistake

Come this way through the wooden gate into our
    garden.
Confront the green tree which once had no identity.
Pluck a leaf. Close your eyes. Smell its acrid odour.
Does it suggest an Oriental dispensary?

One day (after thirteen years) a tree-expert told us
its name: '*Evodia danieli*, without doubt.
From Korea. Odd to find it thriving here in Wales.'
We thanked him. Now we had something to boast
    about.

When visitors came we offered them a leaf proudly.
'Breathe this in,' we'd urge. 'It's rare as Welsh gold.'
Our olfactory gift, our pagan benediction.
'From Korea,' we'd swank. 'It'll charm away your
    cold.'

Who, in all of Great Britain, possessed such treasure?
But then came the summer of the drought. Tired of
    lies
the parched tree suddenly asserted itself, sprouted
ordinary walnuts, shamelessly free of disguise.

Spiked

Meteorite fall, gunshot echo,
ear parasites, who knows what
set those whales gargling to the shore
while promenade voices fussed.
'Whalebone whales,' cried the professor,
'each as long as a cricket pitch,
not seen in the Bristol Channel
before. Yes, the Balaenidae,
distinguished by absence of teeth.'

'As I am, see,' said Dai, 'though I
ate whale-steak once during the war.'
And added, clever, 'Whales for the Welsh.'
Then surprised, and surprising us,
flopped salt-faced, moaning to the floor.
At once a tall staring psychopomp
bolted fast as an ambulance,
mouth open, eyes wild, while others,
different sizes, stampeded too.

In each village, the curtains twitched
as straggling sleep-runners struggled
after the psychopomp. Too late:
at lighting-up time doleful foghorns
blurted and soon sea-mists landed
rapidly, advanced over rocks,
up cliffs, deleted sheep-fields, deep
lanes, and those runners who took the wrong
minor road to Llantwit Major.

That night, night of the avenging whales,
I sent my report typed tidy
to *The Glamorgan Herald*.
I headlined it FARRAGO IN FLIGHT
and THEY FOLLOWED THE PSYCHOPOMP.
Nice. Rhythmic. But the editor said,
'No, mun, no – this incident is of
bugger-all human interest.
Besides, what happened to the whales?'

In the Welsh National Museum

(To Josef Herman)

Josef, in your thaumaturgic studio,
long live cobalt blue and brown!
Autumn is your season,
twilight is your hour.

Now, in my hometown, you, spooky,
conjure up, abracadabra,
this melancholy impostor
who steals my name.

Is he listening to someone
beyond the picture's frame,
playing a Chopin piano
of autumnal unhappiness?

Josef, this other is not me.
This golem hardly looks like me.
Is this your unbegotten brother
lost in menstrual blood?

If so, his passport (forged)
would have been Polish,
his exile inevitable,
his wound undescribable.

Look! My best brown coat
not yet patched at the elbow,
my cobalt blue shirt
not yet frayed at the collar.

As if challenged he, dire,
(Passport? Colour of wound?)
stares back – that look of loss –
at whomsoever stares at him.

Or across at Augustus John's
too respectable W.H. Davies,

at prettified Dylan Thomas
whose lips pout for a kiss.

Infelicitous! Wrong! Impostors
spellbound, enslaved in their world,
with no *emeth* on their foreheads,
without speech, without pneuma.

But the Welsh say, 'Whoever stares long
at his portrait will, with dismay, see
the devil.' So who's wearing my clothes?
Josef, I know your magic. I'll not stay.

In Llandough Hospital

'To hasten night would be humane.'
I, a doctor, beg a doctor,
for still the darkness will not come –
his sunset slow, his first star pain.

I plead: 'We know another law.
For one maimed bird we'd do as much,
and if a creature need not suffer
must he, for etiquette, endure?'

Earlier, 'Go now, son,' my father said,
for my sake commanding me.
Now, since death makes victims of us all,
he's thin as Auschwitz in that bed.

Still his courage startles me. The fears
I'd have, he has none. Who'd save
Socrates from the hemlock,
or Winkelried from the spears?

We quote or misquote in defeat,
in life, and at the camps of death.
Here comes the night with all its stars,
bright butchers' hooks for man and meat.

I grasp his hand so fine, so mild,
which still is warm surprisingly,
not a handshake either, father,
but as I used to when a child.

And as a child can't comprehend
what germinates philosophy,
so like a child I question why
night with stars, then night without end.

Case History

'Most Welshmen are worthless,
an inferior breed, doctor.'
He did not know I was Welsh.
Then he praised the architects
of the German death-camps –
did not know I was a Jew.
He called liberals, 'White blacks',
and continued to invent curses.

When I palpated his liver
I felt the soft liver of Goering;
when I lifted my stethoscope
I heard the heartbeats of Himmler;
when I read his encephalograph
I thought, *'Sieg heil, mein Führer.'*

In the clinic's dispensary
red berry of black bryony,
cowbane, deadly nightshade, deathcap.
Yet I prescribed for him
as if he were my brother.

Later that night I must have slept
on my arm: momentarily
my right hand lost its cunning.

In the Theatre

(A true incident)

'Only a local anaesthetic was given because of the blood pressure problem. The patient, thus, was fully awake throughout the operation, but in those days – in 1938, in Cardiff, when I was Lambert Rogers' dresser – they could not locate a brain tumour with precision. Too much normal brain tissue was destroyed as the surgeon crudely searched for it, before he felt the resistance of it ... all somewhat hit and miss. One operation I shall never forget ...' – Dr Wilfred Abse

Sister saying – 'Soon you'll be back in the ward,'
sister thinking – 'Only two more on the list,'
the patient saying – 'Thank you, I feel fine';
small voices, small lies, nothing untoward,
though, soon, he would blink again and again
because of the fingers of Lambert Rogers,
rash as blind man's, inside his soft brain.

If items of horror can make a man laugh
then laugh at this: one hour later, the growth
still undiscovered, ticking its own wild time;
more brain mashed because of the probe's braille path;
Lambert Rogers desperate, fingering still;
his dresser thinking, 'Christ! Two more on the list,
a cisternal puncture and a neural cyst.'

Then, suddenly, the cracked record in the brain,
a ventriloquist voice that cried, 'You sod,
leave my soul alone, leave my soul alone,' –
the patient's dummy lips moving to that refrain,
the patient's eyes too wide. And, shocked,
Lambert Rogers drawing out the probe
with nurses, students, sister, petrified.

'Leave my soul alone, leave my soul alone,'
that voice so arctic and that cry so odd
had nowhere else to go – till the antique
gramophone wound down and the words began
to blur and slow, '... leave ... my ... soul ... alone ...'
to cease at last when something other died.
And silence matched the silence under snow.

A Prescription

Sweet-tempered, pestering
young man of Oxford
juggling with ghazals,
tercets, haikus, tankas,
not to mention villanelles,
terzanelles and rondelets;
conversant with the phonetic
kinships of rhyme, assonance
and consonance; the four
nuances of stress, the three
junctions; forget now
the skeltonic couplet,
the heroic couplet, the split
couplet, the poulter's measure;
speak not of englyn
penfyr, englyn milwr;
but westward hasten
to that rising, lonely ground
between the evening rivers,
the alder-gazing rivers,
Mawddach and Dysynni.

Let it be dark when, alone,
you climb the awful mountain
so that you can count the stars.
Ignore the giant shufflings
behind you – put out that torch! –
the far intermittent cries
of the nocturnal birds
– if birds they are –
their small screams of torture.
Instead, scholar as you are,
remark the old proverb
how the one who ascends
Cadair Idris at night
comes back in dawn's light
lately mad or a great poet.
Meanwhile, I'll wait here
in this dull room of urine-

flask, weighing-machine,
examination-couch, X-ray screen,
for your return (triumphant
or bizarre) patiently.

The Silence of Tudor Evans

Gwen Evans, singer and trainer of singers,
    who, in 1941, warbled
an encore (Trees) at Porthcawl Pavilion
    lay in bed, not half her weight and dying.
Her husband, Tudor, drew the noise of curtains.

Then, in the artificial dark, she whispered,
    'Please send for Professor Mandlebaum.'
She raised her head pleadingly from the pillow,
    her horror-movie eyes thyrotoxic.
'Who?' Tudor asked, remembering, remembering.

Not Mandlebaum, not that renowned professor
    whom Gwen had once met on holiday;
not that lithe ex-Wimbledon tennis player
    and author of *Mediastinal Tumours*;
not that swine Mandlebaum of 1941?

Mandlebaum doodled in his hotel bedroom.
    For years he had been in speechless sloth,
but now for Gwen and old times' sake he, first-class,
    alert, left echoing Paddington for
a darkened sickroom and two large searching eyes.

She sobbed when he gently took her hand in his.
    'But, my dear, why are you crying?'
'Because, Max, you're quite unrecognizable.'
    'I can't scold you for crying about that,'
said Mandlebaum and he, too, began to weep.

They wept together (and Tudor closed his eyes)
    Gwen, singer and trainer of singers,
because she was dying; and he, Mandlebaum,
    ex-physician and ex-tennis player,
because he had become so ugly and so old.

Sons

Sarcastic sons slam front doors.
  So a far door slams and I think
of Cardiff outskirts where, once, captured acres played
at being small tamed gardens: the concrete way
roads supplanted grass, wild flowers, bosky paths.
Now my son is like that, altering every day.

  I was like that; also like
  those new semis that seemed ashamed,
their naked windows slashed across by whitewash.
At the frontier of Nowhere order and chaos clash.
And who's not lived at the frontier of Nowhere
and being adolescent was both prim and brash?

  Strange a London door should slam
  and I think thus, of Cardiff evenings
trying to rain, of quick dark where raw brick could hide,
could dream of being ruins where ghosts abide.
Still, spreading lamps assert themselves too early.
Awkward Anglo-Welsh half town, half countryside.

  Son, you are like that and I
  love you for it. In adult rooms
the hesitant sense of not belonging quite.
Too soon maturity will switch off your night,
thrust fake electric roots, the nameless becoming
wrongly named and your savage darkness bright.

Imitations

In this house, in this afternoon room,
my son and I. The other side of glass
snowflakes whitewash the shed roof and the grass
this surprised April. My son is 16,
an approximate man. He is my chameleon,
my soft diamond, my deciduous evergreen.

Eyes half closed, he listens to pop forgeries
of music – how hard it is to know – and perhaps
dreams of some school Juliet I don't know.
Meanwhile, beyond the bending window,
gusting suddenly, despite a sky half blue,
a blur of white blossom, whiter snow.

And I stare, oh immortal springtime, till
I'm elsewhere and the age my cool son is,
my father alive again (I, his duplicate)
his high breath, my low breath, sticking to the glass
while two white butterflies stumble, held each
to each, as if by elastic, and pass.

Two Photographs

Here's a photograph of grandmother, Annabella.
How slim she appears, how vulnerable. Pretty.
And here's a photograph of grandmother, Doris.
How portly she looks, formidable. Handsome.
Annabella wears a demure black frock with an amber
    brooch.

Doris, a lacy black gown with a string of pearls.
One photo's marked *Ystalyfera* 1880,
the other *Bridgend* 1890.
Both were told to say, 'Cheese'; one, defiant, said 'Chalk!'

Annabella spoke Welsh with a Patagonian accent.
Doris spoke English with a Welsh Valleys' lilt.
Annabella fasted – pious, passive, enjoyed small-talk.
Doris feasted – pacy, pushy, would never pray. Ate pork!
When Annabella told Doris she was damned
indecorous Doris devilishly laughed.
I liked Doris, I liked Annabella,
though Doris was bossy and Annabella daft.
I do not think they liked each other.

Last night I dreamed they stood back to back,
not for the commencement of a duel
but to see who was taller! Now, in these revived
waking hours, my Eau de Cologne grandmothers
with buns of grey hair, of withered rose,
seem illusory, fugitive, like my dream –
or like the dust that secretively flows
in a sudden sunbeam (sieved through leaky curtains)
and disappears when and where that sunbeam goes.

Of two old ladies once uxoriously loved,
what's survived? An amber brooch, a string of pearls,
two photographs. Happening on them, my children's
grandchildren will ask 'Who?' – hardly aware
that if this be not true, I never lived.

Cousin Sidney

Dull as a bat, said my mother
of cousin Sidney in 1940 that time he tried
to break his garden swing, jumping on it,
size 12 shoes – at fifteen the tallest boy
in the class, taller than loping Dan Morgan
when Dan Morgan wore his father's top hat.

Duller than a bat, said my father
when hero Sidney lied about his age
to claim rough khaki, silly ass;
and soon, somewhere near Dunkirk,
some foreign corner was forever Sidney
though uncle would not believe it.

Missing not dead please God, please,
he said, and never bolted the front door,
never string taken from the letter box,
never the hall light off lest his one son
came home through a night of sleet
whistling, We'll meet again.

Aunt crying and raw in the onion air
of the garden (the unswinging empty swing)
her words on a stretched leash
while uncle shouted, Bloody Germans.
And on November 11th, two howls
of silence even after three decades

till last year, their last year,
when uncle and aunt also went missing,
missing alas, so that now strangers
have bolted their door and cut the string
and no-one at all (the hall so dark)
waits up for Sidney, silly ass.

The Death of Aunt Alice

Aunt Alice's funeral was orderly,
each mourner correct, dressed in decent black,
not one balding relative berserk with an axe.
Poor Alice, where's your opera-ending?
For alive you relished high catastrophe,
your bible Page One of a newspaper.

You talked of typhoid when we sat to eat;
Fords on the M4, mangled, upside down,
just when we were going for a spin;
and, at London airport, as you waved us off,
how you fatigued us with 'metal fatigue',
vague shapes of Boeings bubbling under seas.

Such disguises and such transformations!
Even trees were but factories for coffins,
rose bushes decoys to rip boys' eyes with thorns.
Sparrows became vampires, spiders had designs,
and your friends also grew SPECTACULAR,
none to bore you by dying naturally.

A. had both kidneys removed in error
at Guy's. 'And such a clever surgeon too.'
B., one night, fell screaming down a liftshaft.
'Poor fellow, he never had a head for heights.'
C., so witty, so feminine, 'Pity
she ended up in a concrete-mixer.'

But now, never again, Alice, will you utter
gory admonitions as some do oaths.
Disasters that lit your eyes will no more
unless, trembling up there, pale saints listen
to details of their bloody martyrdoms,
all their tall stories, your eternity.

Uncle Isidore

When I observe a toothless ex-violinist,
with more hair than face, sprawled like Karl Marx
on a park seat or slumped, dead or asleep,
in the central heat of a public library,
I think of Uncle Isidore – smelly
schnorrer and lemon-tea bolshevik – my foreign
distant relative, not always distant.

Before Auschwitz, Treblinka, he seemed near,
those days of local pogroms, five year programmes,
until I heard him say, 'Master, Master
of the Universe, blessed be your name,
don't you know there's been no rain for years
and your people are thirsty? Have you no shame,
compassion? Don't you care at all?'

And fitting the violin to his beard
he bitterly asked me – no philosopher
but a mere boy – 'What difference between
the silence of God and the silence of men?'
Then, distant, as if in the land of Uz,
the answering sky let fall the beautiful
evening sound of thunder and of serious rain.

That was the first time Uncle went lame,
the first time the doctor came and quit hopelessly.
His right foot raised oddly to his left knee,
some notes wrong, all notes wild, unbalanced,
he played and he played not to that small child
who, big-eyed, listened – but to the Master
of the Universe, blessed be his name.

A Winter Visit

Now she's ninety I walk through the local park
where, too cold, the usual peacocks do not screech
and neighbouring lights come on before it's dark.

Dare I affirm to her, so agèd and so frail,
that from one pale dot of peacock's sperm
spring forth all the colours of a peacock's tail?

I do. But she like the sibyl says, 'I would die';
then complains, 'This winter I'm half dead, son.'
And because it's true I want to cry.

Yet must not (although only Nothing keeps)
for I inhabit a white coat not a black
even here – and am not qualified to weep.

So I speak of small approximate things,
of how I saw, in the park, four flamingoes
standing, one-legged on ice, heads beneath wings.

Last Visit to 198 Cathedral Road

When, like a burglar, I entered after dark
the ground-floor flat, I don't know why I sat
in the dark, in my father's armchair,
or why, suddenly, with surgeon's pocket-torch
I hosed the objects of the living room
with its freakish light.

Living room, did I say? Dying room, rather.
So much dust, mother! Outraged, the awakened
empty fruit bowl; the four-legged table
in a fright; the vase that yawned hideously;
the pattern that ran up the curtain, took flight
to the long, wriggling, photophobic crack
in the ceiling.

Omnipotent, I returned them to the dark,
sat sightless in the room that was out
of breath and listened, that summer night,
to Nothing.

Not a fly the Z side of the windowpane,
not one, comforting, diminutive sound
when the silence calmed, became profound.

Progress

Men are up the pole at Ogmore-by-Sea
    replacing five wires with one.
Goodbye musical notes, sweet jamboree.
    Soon the birds of Ogmore will come to the new
thick cable. They'll sing in monotone.

Quests

To reach the other world some sought hemlock
in waste places: umbels of that small white flower
    still sway at eye-level when the eye is still;

    and some, at broad sunset, walked the sea-shore
or prayed for their messiah in a darkening house.
    But gods had human faces and were flawed.

When prying Apion, with eerie conch,
summoned Homer's spirit to ask where he was born
    whose bloody head appeared above the parapet?

    Now at Cardiff, in its shut museum,
a sculptured satyr on a sculptured sea-horse
    blows only silent zeros through his horn.

    And here, in Ogmore, more abundant silence.
Awesome over the sea, from which no sulking Proteus
    will rise, the candled stars, the unblinking moon.

    Who knows? Not me. Secular, I'll never hear
the spheres, their perfect orchestra, or below,
    with joy, old Triton playing out of tune.

At Ogmore-by-Sea this August Evening

I think of one who loved this estuary –
my father – who, self-taught, scraped upon
an obstinate violin. Now, in a room
darker than the darkening evening outside,
I choose a solemn record, listen to
a violinist inhabit a Bach partita.
This violinist and violin are unified.

Such power! The music summons night. What more?
It's twenty minutes later into August
before the gaudy sun sinks to Australia.
Now nearer than the promontory paw
and wincing electric of Porthcawl
look! the death-boat black as anthracite,
at its spotlit prow a pale familiar.

Father? Here I am, Father. I see you
jubilantly lit, an ordered carnival.
The tide's in. From Nash Point no foghorns howl.
I'm at your favourite place where once you held
a bending rod and taught me how to bait
the ragworm hooks. Here, Father, here, tonight
we'll catch a bass or two, or dabs, or cod.

Senseless conjuration! I wipe my smile away
for now, lit at the prow, not my father
but his skeleton stands. The spotlight fails,
the occult boat's a smudge while three far lighthouses
converse in dotty exclamation marks.
The ciaccona's over, the record played,
there's nothing but the tumult of the sea.

A Letter From Ogmore

Goodbye, 20th Century.
What should I mourn?
Hiroshima? Auschwitz?
Our friend, Carmi, said,
'Thank forgetfulness
else we could not live;
thank memory
else we'd have no life.'

Goodbye, 20th Century.
What shall I celebrate?
Darling, I'm out of date:
even my nostalgia
is becoming history.
Those garish, come-on posters
outside a cinema,
announce the Famous
I've never heard of.
So many other friends, too,
now like Carmi, have joined
a genealogy of ghosts.

But here, this mellow evening,
on these high cliffs I look down
to read the unrolling
holy scrolls of the sea. They are
blank. The enigma is alive
and, for the Present, I boast,
thumbs in lapels, I survive.

Delightful Eros
still hauls Reason along
zig-zag on a taut leash.
I'm still unsettled by
the silence in framed pictures,
foreground and background;
or the mastery of music
over mind. And I hail
the world within a word.

I do not need to be
a fabulist like Iolo
who, from this same coast,
would see seven sails
where there was but one.

Goodbye, 20th Century,
your trumpets and your drums,
your war-wounds still unhealed.
Goodbye, I-must-leave-you-Dolly,
goodbye Lily Marlene.
Has the Past always a future?
Will there always be
a jackboot on the stair
a refugee to roam?
A man with no roots is lost
like the darkness in the forest
and it costs 100 years
for a hiding place
to become a home.

Now secular strangers come
sealed in Fords and Nissans,
a congregation of cars,
to this opening estuary
so various, so beautiful, so old.
The tide is out.
And from the sleeping reeled-
in sea – not from
the human mind's vexed fathoms –
the eternal, murderous,
fanged Tusker Rock is revealed.

A Wall

in a field in the County of Glamorgan.
You won't find it named in any guidebook.
It lies, plonk, in the middle of rising ground,
forty-four paces long, high as your eyes,
it begins for no reason, ends no place.
No other walls are adjacent to it.
Seemingly unremarkable, it's just there,
stones of different sizes, different greys.

Don't say this wall is useless, that the grass
on the shadow side is much like the other.
It exists for golden lichens to settle,
for butterflies in their obstacle race
chasing each other to the winning post,
for huddling sheep in a slanting rainfall,
for you to say, 'This wall is beautiful.'

A Figure of 8

In Mr Theophilus's jail
of the sun-striped classroom
the boy half listens to a story
of royalty-loving Christopher Robin.
Then, after musical scales
(his friend, Fatty Jones, is scolded –
Fatty Jones is sobbing),
sings, 'Let the prairie echo,
God bless the Prince of Wales!'

Free, at last, arms horizontal,
he jet-roars out of school
into a vigorous sunset,
soars between the Hs
of the Millennium Stadium,
loops the loop, flies to Africa
to see naked women
(whom gently he caresses);
turns left at Albany Road,
farts H_2Ss.

The evening's shot down in flames
butcher's reds in the clouds are dark,
smoke is rising from the drains,
someone has bombed the park.

Both the swings are on fire,
the empty see-saw is charred;
the enemy is a brute,
the enemy must be foiled;
blood is streaming down the chute,
the wooden horses are running wild.

There's a furnace in the churchyard
(a sorcerer has cast his spell)
the mandrake's screaming and the yew,
the graves are sinking down to hell.

Unseen, a spaceship from another world
flees the heights, drags a spooky trace.
Below, the pond is poisoned and the dew.
Safely the boy comes home to base.

There beneath the night's first star,
observed by his patient cat,
he chalks across the garden shed
FUCK WINNIE THE POOH.
Then adds for luck and Fatty Jones
FUCK MR THEOPHILUS TOO.

The Story of Lazarus

After the war he settled in kindly Cardiff
his English uncertain, his Welsh not at all.
For three years a clerk who hardly said a word.

Then, accusingly, he showed us the number
on his arm, spoke of how he had survived
in his chemistry, the sudden sound of
his heartbeat. Each stark detail. We were shocked.

Week after week this man's monstrous story
heard in Whitchurch, Llandaf, Canton, Cathays,
in pubs and clubs – The Three Elms, The Conway,
The Golden Shark, the Post House, the Moat House;
told even to Cardiff's patient statues:
John Batchelor, Lloyd George, Nye Bevan.

We closed our eyes till we, too, became stone.

So he whispered his dark story to our children
and years later to our children's children.
Soon they merely nodded, eager to join
the procession banging its way outside
to the Firework Display above Roath Park,
the oompha, oompha, down the street fading.

My Cousin, the Soldier

When my cousin, the soldier, returned,
no showers of paper fluttered downwards,
no flags were strung across the street.

At his house no energetic Dalmatian
came bounding out, wagging its tail.
But they say a stranger stepped in front of him
on the front path, took out a key,
and opened the front door. Closed it.

They say my cousin, the soldier, stood still,
observed the front room's surprising curtains;
looked to the right – the neighbour was cutting a hedge,
looked to the left – the traffic lights changed.

I've never believed such stories.
I still don't believe in them.
I remember my cousin, the soldier.
When he was a child he would sleep
with his eyes and mouth wide open like a dead fish.

Terrible Angels

One bedtime, my father showed me his war medals,
their pretty coloured ribbons, and told me
the other story about the angels of Mons,
that élite and puissant expedition from God:
how first their invisible presence caused horses
to bolt and flocks of meat-snatching birds to rise,
circle around and around like a carousel.

But war coarsens (he said) even genteel angels.
When they spoke it was the silence of gas, amen;
when they sang it was shrapnel striking helmets;
then, finally, soldiers' prayers and soldiers' screams
thrilled the cold angels to steal the muskets
of the dead, to become stealthily visible,
bold and bloodthirsty, true facsimiles of men.

(My father, invalided home, was told
he knew more about angels than was healthy.)

Blond Boys

In Stockholm
I saw my first shy love hobble by
hand in hand with her small blond grandson.

Eva Jones, remember me?
My acne. Your dimples.

When your rode your important Raleigh bike
to school, your skirt high,
I held my breath.

With heroic intensity of a 15 year old,
dared by you, I climbed the glass-crowned wall
and stole Mrs Humphreys' summer apples.

Oh the forever of an August Sunday evening
when near the back door's delinquent scent
of honeysuckle, forehead to forehead
I searched your searching eyes.

All the next week similitudes of love,
the jailer of reason,

until plain as the prose of a synopsis,
you bluntly said (with impressive sighs)
'You have a beautiful classy mind
but I find you physically unattractive –
and I prefer, um, blond boys besides.'

Phone Call at Ogmore-by-Sea

At 3 a.m., the hour of the rising Dead,
Hello, Hello? No-one spoke.

Beyond the limits of the ordinary
a stranger would have stood, skull to toe,
transfixed in the doorway
like a lit enlarged Xray film!

Hello? Hello? I wait and know
the intimidation of silence.

       Discharged
from the lunatic asylum of sleep,
now alert, adrenal, I explore
the moonstruck window.

Outside, the sighing, fussy
surge of the sea swarming up
the unpeopled, pebbled shore.

Certain nights the house creaks
and the nearer I move to the dead hour
the smaller I become.

I've eaten my prunes, Daddy.
I've taken my cod-liver oil.

The clock's disarmed.
The night-bird is flying to the moon

and wind and cloud play lighting tricks
above the inebriated-dancing sea
that flaunts mock silver on its blacks.

Dylan

(At the Poetry Library, London, 9th November 2003)

I put down my glass of white wine chilled
to unveil his eyeless staring head.
A heard silence. A stone dropped down a well.

Speeches. His lust for the arson of the word;
his impecunious life like water spilled
from a cupped hand; how Fame advanced spotlit,
wearing jewels over her sores; how her pimp
whispered, 'Dilly, Dilly come and be killed.'

Iolo Morganwg

I, Ellis Owen, antiquary and stone epitaph
    versifier,
testify this morning of February 29th, 1856,
that at Madam Totti's Wednesday night seance
widow Gweneth Jones, scrubber of germs and
    humbug,
dared to ask in the tricks and shivers of
    candlelight,
'Where are you now, you rogue, Iolo Morganwg?'

What a shuffling silence! No disordered
    valediction
from the best poet ever to have languished
in Cardiff Gaol; no protesting squeak at all
from our druid-conceiver, our most loud
    tremendous liar
for whom each Bristol Channel porpoise became
    a whale;
no Welsh Red Indian curses – not a single
    scoffing word
from Iolo who faked and forged great Dafydd's
    verses
– he transcribed one, then invented seven –

until we heard his alto voice, sweet as syrup,
    saying,
'My dear Mrs Jones, my sugar lump, my hazelnut,
here I am, my old snowdrop. Here in Heaven.'

A Welsh Peace Offering

My dear felonious invective swine,
though you have often boggled me,
though I am a bard and you a mere jongleur,
I am mindful of this holy season.

I doubt if *you* are familiar with the story
of the two 14th-century poets,
Dafydd ap Rhys and Hywel ab Ifan
who did not wish each other well.

Dafydd scorned mead-boozed Hywel's clichés.
Hywel sneered, 'Dafydd has two duff ears.'
Each recommended the other's verses:
'A cure certain for insomnia.'

But when one was told the other had died,
by Ieuan of the drooping eyelids (ptosis),
inveterate windbag and practical joker,
both hurried home to swank their best black.

Dafydd composed a seventy-line cywydd
in honour of Hywel and the Nation's loss:
'Dead, dead, our master of the perfect metre.
Ashes, ashes, that blazing fire of a man.'

Hywel, too, played weeping harp notes in praise
of Dafydd, matchless poet, 'O how his lyrics
harmoniously soar, bible-beautiful.
An eagle's feather he did write with.'

Hoaxed terribly they were but stirred by
each other's buttered obituary
they became true friends, close as two sides
of a sandwich – as I hope we shall be.

Still I have to tell you (must be honest)
that your voice resembles an idiot tin can

animated by a relentless wind scraping
and bucketing across the road to Builth.

No matter, it's in the genes, can't be helped.
Now I send this instead of a Xmas card
confident discord between us will cease.

At Caerleon

This shadowy spring evening,
in these ruins of Caerleon,
I hear the alarm of distant shouts.
Soon the skinhead knights
of The Round Table gang appear.
Bored, they horse around, frab,
and throw empty cans of beer
at each other.

The scarred and tattooed
loudest lout
seems to be their King.
The long knife in his buskin
is as keen as Arthur's sword.

Deprived, they bully language
into oaths
until, suddenly, together,
as if a starting gun had sounded,
the outcast, broiling yobs depart
to seek another gang to cull.

A smear of blood on a silken flag,
a golden crown on a decaying skull,
a lust for heroes,
this is where the legends start.
And I'm alone at last,
can lose my reason,
sit upon a stone and play
(paper on a comb) a mournful tune
from an imagined country
that would break an exile's heart,
or summon silhouettes like phantoms
who were coming,
came and now have passed.

On the Coast Road

This ash-end of the year, too short of light,
the grumpy afternoon closes down
and a bossy wind summons, like a conductor,
choirs of ghosts to the telegraph wires.

Soon the roofs of Ogmore recede out of sight
as I walk on awake in the wrong weather.
Ahead, a seagull squeals, bullied off course,
and sheep scrum behind stone-armoured walls.

Tons of air! And nobody on this coast road,
and nobody on the beach below where
the thaumaturge sea thrashes the rocks
and hey-hey presto, fakes fountains of snow.

Down there, on that rock's pulpit, my father fished
till his own days grew shorter. Now, briefly,
this road leads to the Past. Is it the scolding wind
that makes my teeth ache and my eyes water?

At the old, shut farmhouse, I meet a boozy gang
in fancy dress. The man in a white sheet
holds up, on a pole, the skull of a horse.
The Mari Lwyd! I blink. They vanish of course

and the graffito I, as a boy, once chalked
on the ruined barn beyond this farmhouse
has vanished too: STRAIGHT ON FOR THE FUTURE.
Quick, bird, quick, present winds shake the lamp-posts

into staring light. As if pursued, a tin can
buckets past me, scrapes the bleak macadam,
its off-key tinkle diminishing plaintively
with each forward struggling step I take.

The Dog at Ogmore-by-Sea

I walk towards the arena of a sunset.
In shock, a few blood-filled clouds
hardly move before the golden background
of a Sienese painting.

One mile out, Tusker Rock – debased,
Jack-tar black, insanely rises
impatient to devour a ship again
like *The Marryat* or *The Mellany*.

The weekenders have driven home,
the gulls have flown to their dormitory.
Only a queer motionless dog
faces the fuss of the funeral-paced
night-inhabited sea.

The dog, attentive to Time's visible
pomp and majestic progress,
is not waiting for anyone.
His master, if he has a master,
is not in a fogbound ship far away,
sinking down down to Tartarus.

Across the Bay shore lights appear, glow.
I twist my wrist. Of course my watch is round.
Soon the moon must rise open-mouthed,
amazed by its faked splendours below.

Already the purpural sky surrenders
its swags of gold into the thieving sea,
and Time's daylight robbery angers the dog
that does not know it is a dog –
its jaw upraised, its crazed eyes
blaze with merciless gold
and it begins to howl eerily.

At the Concert

Only yesterday while walking on Ogmore cliffs
one listless sheep gave me the yellow eye.
Its jaws moved sideways, munching over and over.
The same old grass. Same old flavour.

I strolled inland and saw the big brown horse
in Lol's sloping field. It stood utterly still.
When I returned it hadn't moved an inch.
It must have been as bored as any statue.

And here's a pretty Miss next to me, motionless.
She'll sit in Row G unawakened by
the conductor's sudden convulsions till
the very last note like a Prince's kiss.

And how's your life? Static too? Do you wait,
as I do, numb, for something to happen
until it happens? If so, join the queue.
It stretches all the way to the Old People's Home.

I'm thinking all this, I mean about the sheep
and the horse, about you and about me
as I pretend to listen to Klump's new free-form
yawn-fecund 'Machine of Dissonances'.

What else can I do except try not to cough
while my cat back home squats in my chair
unmolested, deigning to blink now and then –
at the soundless blank TV screen? I wish

I was there, staring through the garden window
at the pear tree blossoming a masquerade
of snow, an epiphany. No wonder now
Miss is clapping too and someone shouts 'Bravo.'

Postcard to his Wife

Wish you were here. It's a calm summer's day
and the dulcamara of memory
is not enough. I confess without you
I know the impoverishment of self
and the Venus de Milo is only stone.

So come home. The bed's too big! Make excuses.
Hint we are agents in an obscure drama
and must go North to climb 2000 feet
up the cliffs of Craig y Llyn to read
some cryptic message on the face of a rock.

Anything! But come home. Then we'll motor,
just you, just me, through the dominion
of Silurian cornfields, follow the whim
of twisting narrow lanes where hedges
have wild business with roses and clematis.

Or we could saunter to the hunkered blond
sand dunes and, blessed, mimic the old gods
who enacted the happy way to be holy.
Meanwhile, dear, your husband is so uxorious
absence can't make Abse's heart grow fonder.

The Malham Bird

(For Joan)

That long summer a clarity of marvels
yet no morning News announced the great world
had been reinvented and we were new,
in love – you a Gentile and I a Jew!

Dear wife, remember our first illicit
holiday, the rented room, the hidden beach
in Wales, the tame seagull that seemed a portent,
a love message, as if Dafydd's ghost had sent it?

After our swim we lay on our shadows naked,
more than together, and saw high in the blue
two chalk lines kiss and slowly disappear.
Then the friendly gull swooped down, magnified, near.

Now, three grandchildren later, I think of
a black feathered bird, the malham of Eden,
how it took advice, closed its eyes resolute,
when others singing pecked forbidden fruit;

and how, of all the birds, it was not banished
but stayed, lonely, immortal, forever winging
over the vanished gardens of Paradise.

A Scene from Married Life

That unseasonable July in Ogmore
nothing was happening until it happened,
the commuters trapped in their stuffy office block,
the sea slow, the Monday beach sullen, empty,

and I, thinking of the squabble with my wife:
fast barbed words that made the other squirm
and fed flushed indignation, verbal revenge –
a dead bird eaten by the early worm.

I piled up my usual clothes and daps tidily
on a convenient boulder brooding nearby
and, troubled, saw the far dank confusion of
the sea and sky in resentful wedlock.

A mile out the monstrous Tusker Rock crammed
with ghosts and psychopomps raised black fangs.
So many boats it had torn asunder. Seagulls
drifted above it like lost thoughts of the damned.

Soon, daring the fussy sea, I entered
a B movie to enact my great climactic scene.
(After I sank – weep for me – the credits would come up,
then the screen, appropriately, would go blank.)

I swivelled for a last winsome longshot, saw
on the high cliff my wife dressed in blue and all
the best of the world true and desirable.
With surrendering waves I crawled to the shore.

Our own cold wars during the real Cold War
were few and brief. Sulky, I'd linger at my desk
but children's cries were mightier than the pen.
And sweet the armistice, each kiss, and then...

Dafydd ap Gwilym at Llanbadarn

I don't give a monkey-nut for their prissy talk.
Sunday – forgive me, Lord – is an amiable time
to chase the chaste. After church of course.
But no unburdened smile or sweet kiss ever
from one starched lady of Llanbadarn.
And me, so randy, I can hardly walk.

Give them boils, Lord, since none my needs assuage
– not even she whose nose seems like a chair
for spectacles! I ache. If only one, in luck,
roused me in the heather then Garwy himself
would stagger back envious and awestruck.
Lesbians they must be. Give them pox, Lord, and age.

When, parasolled, they left the church slow-paced
along the gravel pathway, past the grand
shadow of the yew, I winked, I whispered.
Nun-faced they frowned their strait-laced Never!
So I, as true a stud as Garwy stand
near graves, full of sperm. Oh what a waste!

St Valentine's Night

Eros, immutable archer, one eye closed,
you let your arrows fly. It was St Valentine's
night, I remember. For me the first time. The Cardiff
moon was flirting with a cloud, its light discreet,
and I with a box of Black Magic chocolates
and she with such a healthy appetite.

Homage to Eros! Slow and sensual the sweet
unwrapping, the soft-centred she coming into sight.
St Valentine, himself, would have been up
to make love to her, with her fallen party dress
rustling on the rug like classy chocolate paper.

Be with me still, jubilant Eros, life-saver,
necessary ally. The other gods only wound
the world and scowling Thanatos keeps trying
to recite the 11th commandment: Thou shalt die.
It was St Valentine's night, I remember.
You plucked your great bow then, Eros. Pluck it now.

Marzipan. Cherry Liqueur. Turkish Delight.

NOTES

'Musical Moments'

Backslangs: words pronounced backwards.

Jabberwocks: nonsense words, like "brillig" and "slithy", as in Lewis Carroll's 'Jabberwocky' in *Through the Looking Glass*.

Hammond for Hobbs: famous cricketers on cards that were collected and swapped.

Moiseiwitsch: well-known pianist.

Empire: cinema with big stage in Queen Street, Cardiff.

'Horse'

Roman road: the Golden Mile, part of the narrow A48 approaching Bridgend along which the Abse family travelled on their way to Ogmore-by-Sea.

"In the 1930s, when we lived in Cardiff, our car, a Riley, seemed to know only one route. It would go instinctively to Ogmore-by-Sea. My father only had to sit in the driving seat, turn on the ignition, and off it would go along the A48, up Tumble Down Dick, through Cowbridge, up and down Crack Hill, all of the twenty-three miles to the sea, the sea at Ogmore. Every half-sunny Sunday, every holiday, the car knew we wanted to play cricket on the sands of Hardee's Bay while its boss, my father, fished near the mouth of the river for dabs, salmon bass, and ghosts." – *Intermittent Journals*, 147-148.

'Down the M4'

Patagonia: in southern Argentina, to which many Welsh people emigrated between 1865 and 1914. A number of Patagonians still speak Welsh.

Ystalyfera: the village, where Dannie Abse's mother was born and grew up, on the River Tawe north of Swansea.

'Return to Cardiff'

Tiger Bay: the docklands of Cardiff, especially the area around Bute Street. Recently the setting for a TV soap series.

'The Game'

Fred Keenor and *Billy Hardy* played for Cardiff City in 1927, when, before a crowd of 93,000, the Bluebirds won the FA Cup at Wembley.

The white ball: on winter afternoons, with no floodlights, they used a white ball instead of the usual brown.

Ted Drake: Arsenal centre-forward.

Dixie Dean: Everton centre-forward.

Faust: in Marlowe's play, 'Dr Faustus' sells his soul to Mephistopheles but here the poet calls on God to "sign our souls". There are strong hints of religious and spiritual parallels throughout the poem.

"I was nine years of age when I went to Ninian Park for the first time on my own. I watched a game between Cardiff City and Torquay United. Cardiff were floundering near the bottom of Division 3 (South) and it seemed increasingly likely that they would have to bid for re-election at the end of the season. No matter; the spruce military band, with infinite sadness, played the Bluebirds' inappropriate signature, 'Happy Days Are Here Again' as the City team ran from the dark tunnel.

Yesterday Torquay were again visiting Ninian Park and I followed the crowd that converged with sanguine expectation towards the City ground – men and blue-jeaned youths mainly, some wearing blue and white Cardiff City scarves. All walked purposefully in the same direction, past an unhygienic-looking van whose owner purveyed sizzling sausages and onions, past the Ninian pub and the stern, distrustful police, then under the deteriorating railway bridge into Sloper Road with its cloth-capped programme-sellers near the looming Stands and the high unlit floodlights of Ninian Park itself.

In 1933 I, a small boy, had been handed down above a mass of friendly faces from the darkness at the back of the now-demolished Grangetown Stand right to the front, behind the goalposts. There, breathing in neighbouring pipe and Woodbine or Craven A cigarette smoke I could observe, at acrid eye-level, my blue-shirted heroes display their rare skills and common blunders." – *Intermittent Journals*, 199-200.

'Cricket Ball'

Slogger Smart: Cyril Smart used to bat no.6 for Glamorgan. In those days the team played at Cardiff Arms Park; the Angel Hotel is opposite, on the other side of Westgate Street.

'Welsh Valley Cinema, 1930s'

rhonchi: wheezing, sometimes sonorous sounds, caused by air passing through bronchial tubes in the lungs.

silicosis: miner's chest disease.

mecca carpet: because the cinema carpet was so plush and some-times those in the cinema did not have shoes.

glycerine: colourless fluid used to simulate tears on screen.

Woodbine: cheap cigarette.

'Arianrhod'

Arianrhod: in the *Mabinogion*, a beautiful and imprisoned woman, sister of Gwydion and mother of Lleu Llawgyffes who marries Blodeuwedd.

night-war: Swansea had air-raids three nights in succession in 1941.

Bowdler: Thomas Bowdler, the editor of Shakespeare who deleted everything "which cannot with propriety be read aloud to the family", is buried in the graveyard of 'All Saints', Mumbles, Swansea.

'Lament of Heledd'

'Canu Heledd' is one of the longest cycles of saga englynion in the Welsh language. In a deeply tragic poem, Heledd, last of the House of Powys, laments the loss of her home and brothers, especially King Cynddylan. Englynion are the oldest recorded Welsh metrical form. The most popular englyn has four lines and a complex rhythm and rhyme scheme. They can be written as separate poems like haiku, or as links in a chain.

'The Boasts of Hywel ab Owain Gwynedd'

Hywel ab Owain Gwynedd: (d.1170), a prince, poet and soldier, illegitimate son of Owain Gwynedd, was killed in battle against two of his half-brothers. He is remembered particularly as a poet of love.

'Meurig Dafydd to His Mistress'

Meurig Dafydd: born in Cardiff, was a professional gentleman poet to the landed families of Glamorgan and Gwent during the early seventeenth century.

Stradlings: an influential family of St Donat's Castle, Glamorgan.

John Stradling: (d. 1637) the founder of Cowbridge Grammar School, spoke no Welsh and claimed descent from the first Norman conquerors of Glamorgan. He published a number of books of poetry.

Taliesin: late sixth century poet, lived in the Old North of Britain. His work is found in *The Book of Taliesin* and he appears as the subject of the mythological folk tale 'Hanes Taliesin' probably developed during the ninth to tenth centuries. Taliesin is generally recognized as one of the great founders of the Welsh poetic tradition.

Morien, Morial, March: are all heroes mentioned in 'The Stanzas of the Graves' which date from the ninth or tenth century (see *The Oxford Book of Welsh Verse in English* ed. Gwyn Jones, p.13).

Llywelyn the Last: Llywelyn ap Gruffydd (1225-1282), ruler of Gwynedd, by overcoming lesser princes united Wales and was confirmed as Prince of Wales by Henry III. His defeat at the hands of Edward I at the River Irfon near Builth marked the end of the House of Gwynedd and of the fragile Welsh state he had created.

Lewys Glyn Cothi: (1420-89) a Welsh poet of the fifteenth century famous, above all, for his elegies, especially the moving elegy for his son, Siôn y Glyn, who died aged five. Little is known about him but over two hundred of his poems have survived.

Bewpyr (Beaupre) Castle, a medieval manor house near Cowbridge, was remodelled in the sixteenth century in Tudor Gothic/Italian Renaissance style. It belonged to the Bassets.

"I wanted to visit Beaupre because there, after Xmas in 1603, a party took place during which a local bard, Meurig Dafydd (possibly from nearby Pentre Meurig?) eulogised the Squire. Afterwards Meurig Dafydd was asked if he had another copy of the praise-poem. 'No, by my fayth,' sayd the rhymer, 'but I hope to take a copie of that which I delivered to you.' Alas, the poem was then promptly, insultingly, thrown on to the blazing fire.

The castellated Elizabethan ruin of Beaupre is beautifully

situated. From the road we walked through meadows beside the narrow River Thaw to reach its higher, secluded position. Much of the original mansion is still standing. We approached the house through an outer gatehouse and there, in front of us, was a beautiful, decorated porch which beckoned us to pass through. Did I then find the room I was looking for, that long room with its gallery – roofless now, of course? Here, certainly, was a great fireplace; and it was easy to imagine the harpists and lute players above us in the gallery, and the assembly below where we were standing. Surely the fire once blazed in that large grate and the blackened, charred bits of Meurig Dafydd's poem swirled up the chimney while John Stradling, one of the Squire's English guests, a man of letters himself, laughed out loud at Meurig Dafydd's discomfort.

Emyr Humphreys, in his book *The Taliesin Tradition*, is justifiably angry that Meurig Dafydd was so insulted by the Squire and his guests. Humphreys writes, 'The old squire's action was more than a calculated insult. A great deal more than a few lines of alliterative poetry was being thrown away. His gesture was a symbol. An entire class was relinquishing responsibilities that in former times had held the Welsh culture and social fabric together. An aristocratic tradition of more than a thousand years' duration was being tossed "into the fire".' – *Intermittent Journals*, 220-221.

'Elegy for Dylan Thomas'

Emily: Dylan Thomas told the story of how a certain American lady said how much she admired his Hornblower series. When Dylan remarked that C.S. Forester was the author, the lady's husband shouted out "Wrong again, Emily".

collected legends: his *Collected Poems* (1952) had recently been published.

'A Sea-shell for Vernon Watkins'

Pennard: west of Swansea on the Gower coast. Vernon Watkins (1906-1967) moved there in 1931 and lived there for the rest of his life. He worked for Lloyds Bank in Swansea. A close friend of Dylan Thomas, Watkins published nine volumes of poetry strongly influenced by the Gower coastline, and Christian and Platonic beliefs.

'A Heritage'

the god: Pluto, god of the underworld.
Enna: a town in the middle of Sicily on a beautiful plain from
    where Prosperine was carried away by Pluto to be his queen.

'Altercation in Splott"

Splott: southern residential part of Cardiff.

'Assimilation'

The poem is based on a Rabbinic legend which tells what happened when a stranger asked for hospitality in the city of Sodom.

'Spiked'

The poem is based on a true story of a whale that became
stranded in the Ogwr estuary. *Spiked* refers to articles never used
by a newspaper.
psychopomp: a conductor of souls to the place of the dead.

'In the Welsh National Museum'

Josef Herman: born in Poland in 1911, he settled in Britain in
    1940. He lived in Glasgow until 1943 before moving to
    Ystradgynlais, where he became well-known for his portraits
    of miners at work. His later years were spent in London,
    where he died in 2000.
golem: a figure of Kabbalistic legend; a man made originally out
    of clay and mud who cannot speak but obeys commands. On
    the forehead is written *Emeth* (truth). By striking off the E,
    the figure will collapse since *meth* means dead.

"Some years back Josef Herman painted a powerful portrait of
me. He sold it to the gallery of the Welsh National Museum and
when my mother went to have a look at it there – she was then
in her eighties – she made an embarrassing fuss. 'That's not my
son,' she apparently said to everybody within megaphone distance, 'that looks like the devil.' They finally had to call the
curator. Meanwhile she stared at the nearby idealised painting
of Dylan Thomas by Augustus John, all curly hair, all soulful
eyes. My mother seethed. No wonder, soon after, Josef
Herman's portrait was removed to the darkness of the
Museum's store room. As my mother said, 'Now, if Jack had

painted you, you would have looked as nice as Dylan Thomas.'"
– *Intermittent Journals*, 72.

'In Llandough Hospital'

Socrates: (470-399 BC) Athenian Philosopher, teacher of Plato, his moral integrity cost him his life. Brought to trial accused of not worshipping the gods of the state and of corrupting the young, he defended himself but was found guilty (and given the opportunity to propose his own punishment) and sentenced to death. He refused the chance to escape and died by drinking hemlock.

Winkelried: fourteenth century Swiss national hero who rushed bravely upon the pikes of the Austrians, thus helping the Swiss to victory.

'Case History'

my right hand lost its cunning: see *The Book of Psalms*, Psalm 137.

'In the Theatre'

Lambert Rogers: was a leading brain surgeon who practised in the Cardiff Royal Infirmary.

'A Prescription'

ghazal: verse form with recurrent rhyme scheme in Arabic and Persian (there follows a list of different verse forms used in English and Welsh poetry).

poulter's measure: metre of poetry with alternate lines of twelve and fourteen syllables.

'Uncle Isidore'

This poem and 'The Silence of Tudor Evans' both lean on Midrashic writings – the nonlegal part of the Talmud which contains parables, homilies and allegories. For example: Levi ordered a public fast, yet no rain came. He said to God, "Master of the Universe you have gone up and sit on high, and you have no compassion on your children." Then the rain came; but Levi became lame.

'A Winter Visit'

the sibyl: a prophetess. The most famous, the Cumaean sibyl, acted as Aeneas's guide to the underworld and lived for a thousand years.

'Quests'

Apion: "reported in my hearing that he had conjured up spirits to enquire of Homer what country he was born in and from what parents he was descended; but he dared not say what answer was given" (so Pliny reported).

a sculptured satyr: the sculpture referred to in the Welsh National Museum is 'Satyr on a Sea Horse', sixteenth century, school of Riccio.

Proteus, Triton: a reference to Wordsworth's sonnet 'The world is too much with us': "So might I, standing on this pleasant lea, / Have glimpses that would make me less forlorn; / Have sight of Proteus coming from the sea; / or hear old Triton blow his wreathed horn."

'A Letter from Ogmore'

Iolo: Iolo Morganwg (Edward Williams) 1747-1826, born at Llancarfan in the Vale of Glamorgan, worked as a stonemason for most of his life. Influenced by the cultural and antiquarian revival in Wales, he became a poet in both Welsh and English. He invented the Gorsedd (the assembly of Bards) to support the Welsh literary tradition and it has since become an integral part of the Welsh Eisteddfod. Seen as a "fabulist" because of his tendency to romanticise or even alter Welsh literature and history.

So various, so beautiful: a reference to Matthew Arnold's poem 'Dover Beach'.

Tusker Rock: in the Bristol Channel, one mile south of Ogmore-by-Sea, which can be seen when the tide is out.

'A Figure of 8'

Christopher Robin: was the son of AA Milne and the inspiration for the fictional little boy and friend of the teddy bear, Winnie the Pooh, in Milne's Winnie-the-Pooh books, especially 'Winnie-the-Pooh' (1926) and 'The House at Pooh Corner' (1928). The real Christopher Robin named his teddy bear after Winnipeg, a bear in London Zoo.

'God bless the Prince of Wales': song performed in 1863, written to mark the marriage of future King Edward VII to Alexandra of Denmark. Actual words are: 'Oh! Let the prayer re-echo/ God bless the Prince of Wales'.

H_2S: Hydrogen Sulphide and its rotten egg smell.

'Story of Lazarus'

John Batchelor: 1820-83, played an important part in the political and public life of Cardiff. His statue, unveiled 16 October 1886, stands in The Hayes, in the middle of the city, with the inscription 'The Friend of Freedom'. He was a timber merchant and ship-builder, Liberal councillor and Mayor of the city.

Lloyd George: 1863-1945: his statue is in the Gorsedd Gardens in Cathays Park, Cardiff. A Welsh-speaking solicitor from North Wales, he became a Liberal MP in 1890 and Prime Minister from 1916 to 1922. A brilliant politician, nicknamed the Welsh Wizard, he is especially well-known for his 'People's Budget' which introduced old age pensions, unemployment benefit, and state financial support for the needy and so laid the foundations for the welfare state.

Nye Bevan: 'located in Queen Street at its western end, a typically pugnacious statue of Aneurin Bevan, post war labour politician and classic Welsh firebrand' (from 'Wales: The Rough Guide').

'Terrible Angels'

The angels of Mons: these fictional angels appeared in an account by Arthur Machen who described how at the Battle of Mons in August 1914, the ghosts of the Welsh archers of the Battle of Agincourt came to the aid of the British army by loosing their arrows against German positions. Machen's piece appeared in the *London Evening News* and became credited as fact.

'Dylan'

The poem recalls Dylan Thomas's death, said to be the result of an excessive drinking bout, in New York on 9th March, 1953.

The previous year his 'Collected Poems, 1934-1952' had been awarded the Foyle's Poetry Prize.

'Iolo Morganwg'

Dafydd: Dafydd ap Gwilym, 1340-1370, the greatest medieval Welsh poet; his reputation in Welsh poetry is akin to Chaucer's in English poetry. He is particularly well known for his love poems, many of which have been translated into English.

Iolo Morganwg (Edward Williams – see previous note) published a collection of poems he claimed to be by Dafydd ap Gwilym but which were in fact his own.

Ellis Owen: poet and antiquary, 1789-1868, many of his poems were in the form of epitaphs: he is also remembered for an influential literary society which met at his home.

'A Welsh Peace Offering'

Bard: from the Welsh, 'bardd', a poet.

Jongleur: from the French, a wandering poet or minstrel who recited poems in royal courts and noble households.

'At Caerleon'

Caerleon: near Newport, was the site of a large Roman camp founded around AD 75. According to legend, it was also the site of King Arthur's court.

Frab: to harass, worry

'On the Coast Road'

The Mari Lwyd: refers to a Welsh folk custom which still exists in the area around Maesteg, north of Dannie Abse's home in South Wales. The custom centres on a horse's skull carried on a pole which was led from house to house during the Christmas season. The ritual also involved the impromptu exchange of verses between the callers and the householders and the offering of food and drink.

'The Dog at Ogmore-by-Sea'

Tartarus: in Greek mythology, part of the underworld, lower than

Hades, a place of punishment.

'Postcard to his Wife'

Craig y Llyn: Welsh for 'cairn of the lake'; the highest point in the South Wales valleys.

'The Malham Bird'

Dafydd: Dafydd ap Gwilym and his poem Yr Wylan, The Seagull.

According to Jewish legend, the Malham bird of Eden obeyed the commandment not to eat of the forbidden fruit and so lives forever in Paradise. This means that it cannot taste of the joys of this world, such as marriage.

'A Scene from Married Life'

B movie: refers to a film usually made on a low budget and intended as the second, less significant half of the double-feature programmes which were common in the 1950s.

'St Valentine's Night'

Black Magic chocolates: an approach Dannie seems to have got from his father: 'Those occasional Saturday nights my father would buy a rustling box of Black Magic chocolates for my mother and, of course, they would let me dip into it. Marzipan, Turkish Delight, Coffee Cream, Nougat, Cherry Liqueur. I cannot bite now into the dark hearts of such chocolate without experiencing a Proustian evocation of a time and a place and a circumstance.' – *Intermittent Journals*, 246

SELECTED BIBLIOGRAPHY

Poetry
After Every Green Thing (London: Hutchinson, 1948)
Walking Under Water (London: Hutchinson, 1952)
Tenants of the House: Poems 1951-56 (London: Hutchinson, 1957)
Poems, Golders Green (London: Hutchinson, 1962)
A Small Desperation (London: Hutchinson, 1968)
Selected Poems (London: Hutchinson, 1970)
Funland and Other Poems (London: Hutchinson, 1973)
Collected Poems 1948-1976 (London: Hutchinson, 1977)
Way Out In The Centre (London: Hutchinson, 1981)
Ask The Bloody Horse (London: Hutchinson, 1986)
White Coat, Purple Coat: Poems 1948-1988 (London: Hutchinson, 1989)
Remembrance of Crimes Past: Poems 1986-1989 (London: Hutchinson, 1990)
On The Evening Road (London: Hutchinson, 1994)
Arcadia, One Mile (London: Hutchinson, 1998)
New and Collected Poems (London: Hutchinson, 2003)
Running Late (London, Hutchinson) 2006

Novels and Short Stories
Ash on a Young Man's Sleeve (London: Hutchinson, 1954)
Some Corner of an English Field (London: Hutchinson, 1956)
O. Jones, O. Jones (London: Hutchinson, 1970)
There Was a Young Man from Cardiff (Bridgend: Seren, 2001)
The Strange Case of Dr Simmonds and Dr Glas (London: Robson Books, 2002)

Autobiography and other prose
A Poet In The Family (London: Hutchinson, 1974)
A Strong Dose of Myself (London: Hutchinson, 1983)
Journals From The Ant-Heap (London: Hutchinson, 1986)
Intermittent Journals (Bridgend: Seren, 1994)

Goodbye, Twentieth Century (London: Pimlico, 2001)
The Two Roads Taken (London: Enitharmon, 2003)
The Presence (London: Hutchinson, 2007)

Plays
Three Questors Plays (London: Scorpion, 1967)
The View From Row G (Bridgenzd: Seren, 1990)

Critical Essays on Dannie Abse include:
The Poetry of Dannie Abse ed. J. Cohen (London: Robson Books, 1983)
Dannie Abse (Writers of Wales Series) by Tony Curtis (Cardiff: University of Wales Press, 1985)

ACKNOWLEDGEMENTS

Acknowledgements are due to the following magazines for previously uncollected poems ('Welsh Valley Cinema, 1930s'; 'Lament of Heledd'; 'A Heritage'; 'Progress'; 'The Boasts of Hywel ab Owain Gwynedd'; 'Altercation in Splott'; 'Assimilation'; 'Spiked' and 'A Letter From Ogmore'): *London Magazine*, *New Statesman*, *Planet*, *PN Review*, *Poetry Review* and *Poetry Wales*.

The other poems are taken from books published by Hutchinson: *Collected Poems 1948-1976*; *White Coat, Purple Coat: Collected Poems 1948-1988*; *Remembrance of Crimes Past* and *On The Evening Road, Arcadia, One Mile, New and Collected Poems*, and *Running Late*.

AUTHOR NOTE

Born in Cardiff in 1923, Dannie Abse was for many years a chest specialist in a London clinic. A poet, novelist and playwright, he has written and edited more than sixteen books of poetry, as well as books about medicine. He is the author of *Ash on a Young Man's Sleeve* and several autobiographical volumes. His most recent novel, *The Strange Case of Dr Simmonds and Dr Glas*, was longlisted for the Booker Prize in 2002. The following year his *New and Collected Poems* received the Special Commendation of the Poetry Book Society, and his latest book of poetry, *Running Late*, won the Roland Mathias Prize in 2007. Most recently *The Presence*, Abse's response to the sudden death of his wife and portrait of their fifty year marriage, was made Welsh Book of the Year in 2008.

Dannie Abse
A Sourcebook
Edited by Cary Archard

This is an essential companion to the poetry, prose, drama and critical writings of this major author. Cary Archard collects here a marvellous representative selection of Abse's own writings, together with criticism of his work, which illuminates Abse's achievements for both students and general readers.

* Critical introduction
* Selection of Abse's criticism, autobiography and fiction
* Interviews
* Reviews of Abse's poetry over sixty years
* Critical essays of Abse's poetry, some newly commissioned
* Select bibliography

Dannie Abse practised for many years as a doctor in a London chest clinic. Among his many publications are a dozen books of poetry and five novels, the last of which, *The Strange Case of Dr Simmonds and Dr Glas*, was longlisted for the Booker Prize. His book of poems, *Running Late*, won the Roland Mathias Prize and his prose memoir, *The Presence*, was Wales Book of the Year 2008. In 2009, he received the Wilfred Owen Association Poetry Award. His latest poetry collection is *Two For Joy – Scenes from Married Life*.

Cary Archard was editor of *Poetry Wales* from 1981 to 1986. He founded Seren in 1981. He has edited *Alun Lewis: Collected Poems, Alun Lewis: Collected Stories, Poetry Wales: 25 Years* and *Welsh Retrospective*. He is a Chief Examiner at 'A' Level English Literature for the WJEC in Wales.

£14.99 334pp. Available from booksellers or direct from the publisher Seren 57 Nolton Street, Bridgend CF31 3AE 01656 663018
www.serenbooks com